#1 *NEW YORK TIMES* BESTSELLER
THE OBAMA DIARIES

Proving that truth is stranger than fiction!

OBAMA ON SARAH PALIN: "Hell, doesn't Palin have anything better to do than criticize me? Shouldn't she be back home shooting some endangered wolf species from a helicopter?"

MICHELLE ON BEING FIRST LADY: "I'll be damned if all this fabulosity is going to go to waste reading Dr. Seuss to snot-nosed kids all day."

VICE PRESIDENT BIDEN ON MICHELLE OBAMA: "She's kind of like a black Hillary Clinton. I mean that in a good way."

OBAMA ON CHINA'S ERECTION OF THE MISSILE PLANT IN IRAN: "The Chinese have to make a living too! And those missiles can't reach farther than, say, Tel Aviv, so there's nothing to worry about."

OBAMA ON HIS VISIT TO THE VATICAN: "If I can ingratiate myself with a few more of these red-hats, the pope thing might not be a bad follow-up to the presidency."

**This title is also available from Simon & Schuster Audio
and as an eBook**

ALSO BY LAURA INGRAHAM

Power to the People

Shut Up and Sing

The Hillary Trap

LAURA INGRAHAM

THE
OBAMA
DIARIES

THRESHOLD EDITIONS

NEW YORK   LONDON   TORONTO   SYDNEY

Threshold Editions
A Division of Simon & Schuster, Inc.
1230 Avenue of the Americas
New York, NY 10020

First Threshold Editions trade paperback edition June 2011

THRESHOLD EDITIONS and colophon are trademarks
of Simon & Schuster, Inc.

For information about special discounts for bulk purchases,
please contact Simon & Schuster Special Sales at
1-866-506-1949 or business@simonandschuster.com.

The Simon & Schuster Speakers Bureau can bring authors to your live event.
For more information or to book an event contact the Simon & Schuster Speakers
Bureau at 1-866-248-3049 or visit our website at www.simonspeakers.com.

Designed by Ruth Lee Mui

Manufactured in the United States of America

10   9   8   7   6   5   4   3   2   1

Library of Congress Cataloging-in-Publication Data

Ingraham, Laura.
   The Obama diaries / by Laura Ingraham. — 1st Threshold hardcover ed.
      p. cm.
1. Obama, Barack—Humor.   I. Title.
E908.3.I54 2010
973.932020'7—dc22   2010019945

ISBN: 978-1-4391-9751-6
ISBN: 978-1-4391-9845-2 (trade paperback)
ISBN: 978-1-4391-9844-5 (ebook)

For Maria and Dmitri

CONTENTS

INTRODUCTION

You might call what follows the drama behind Obama.

I didn't go looking for what you are about to read; rather in the grand designs of destiny, it found me. On May 20, 2010, I did what I do every Thursday—I treated myself to a pedicure. It was forty-five minutes of sheer uninterrupted bliss, and I left the salon at the Watergate complex feeling relaxed and carefree. The elevator to the underground parking garage was under repair, so I walked the four floors down to retrieve my car. As I pressed the remote to unlock the car door, my eye caught a thick manila envelope lying on the hood of the car. The words "Property of the American People" were scrawled in black Magic Marker on the front. As I cautiously lifted the package, a deep baritone voice called out from the nearby stairwell. "Just read it," he said. "You'll know what to do." Except for his high-top sneakers, his identity was obscured by the shadows.

"Who are you? What is this?!" I shouted back. The mystery man stood silent for a few seconds and then vanished faster than Obama's high approval ratings. Shaking, I threw the envelope in my car, unsure of what I should do next, or where I should go. Being alone did not seem like a good idea, nor did going straight home. So I drove over to the W hotel, maybe a hundred yards from the White House, where the rooftop bar was humming. I ordered a drink, found a little nook, plopped down, and ripped open the envelope. What I found inside took my breath away—literally. For almost two hours, I sat there—oblivious to the loud dance beat booming over the speakers—leafing through the papers, totally transfixed.

In my possession were copies of excerpts from what appeared to be many of President Barack Obama's handwritten "diaries," as well as those of Michelle Obama; her mother, Marian Robinson; Vice President Joe Biden; Rahm Emanuel; David Axelrod, and others. Here was a firsthand account of the Obama presidency, as it happened, in the words of those who shaped it.

One "diary" was more fascinating and more revealing than the next. The intrigue, the emotion, the struggles, the sheer arrogance of these people jumped off the pages. When I finished reading the last entry in the packet, I found myself aching for more. Each installment told us something new and revealing about the personalities in the Obama White House.

As I began to think about what to do with this treasure trove of information, I looked through the bar's floor-to-ceiling windows at the Washington Monument framed in an ethereal orange trim. Just then, I heard Marine One, the president's helicopter, as it rose off the South Lawn of the White House. Inside might have been Barack Obama jaunting off somewhere for the weekend—was he aware that some of his "diaries" had been copied? Was the FBI already on the case? My heart began pounding at the thought of what lay ahead, as I knew these writings would send shock waves through Washington, the country, and the world.

It was then that I decided not to keep the "diaries" for my own personal amusement, but to release them to the public, to share them with others for the good of the country and the world.

I tried to call Bob Woodward, but he wouldn't take my call. Then I attempted to send an e-mail to Matt Drudge, but my air card couldn't find a signal. *Maybe these are signs that I should release the "diaries" myself*, I thought.

Of course, the problem with diaries is that you can never be sure if the author, particularly a public figure, is telling the whole truth or shading it for posterity. Rather than commenting on the "diaries" or vouching for their veracity, I have elected simply to place them in historical context. The "diary" entries are arranged by topic and framed by relevant facts and quotes from the parties involved. I am very free with my opinions about the public record of Team Obama, but thought it best to withhold judgment on the explosive material in the "diaries" and let the authors speak for themselves. Discerning fact from fiction in these "journals" will be up to you. Ultimately, I feel this approach will permit readers to come to their own conclusions about Obama, his intimates, and their designs.

While working on this book and reading these "diaries," I must admit that I had previously overlooked something about the Obamas—they are flippin' hilarious!

It is hard to think of a more self-important president than Barack Obama, and harder to imagine a press corps more willing to prop up his outsize ego. They have created a mythic image of Obama as redeemer—a secular savior virtually beyond reproach. The Obama mythos has been shaped by the repetition of the various superlatives used to describe him: brilliant . . . a phenomenal listener . . . calm under pressure . . . a master communicator . . . empathetic . . . a uniter, not a divider . . . works tirelessly for the American people. They have exalted him above all others.

This deification of the president is one of the biggest con jobs in American political history.

Beneath that elevated chin and that purposely furrowed brow is a man who I believe is truly worthy—worthy of satire, that is. Such arrogance and pomposity screams out for ridicule.

The satiric diaries bring the Obama reality show into clear and frightening focus: the titanic egos . . . the devious plans . . . the stunning incompetence.

As we suffer under the rule of Obama, it's easy to get depressed and discouraged. But before you reach for the Paxil, I want to suggest another path. Take the time to see this president and his administration for what they are: buffoons. Whatever your political bent, put your feet up, and allow our president to fulfill his campaign promise to bring us together: together in hysterical laughter!

I wrote this book because I believe we are at the crossroads of history. In my other books, I warned about the liberal elites who are amassing more and more power over the American people. With the rise of the Obama administration, I fear that we have reached what may be a tipping point, and that we risk a future in which average Americans have less power over their lives than their parents had. Since Obama was sworn into office, Americans have been mobilizing to fight his agenda. With so much at stake, it is important to see all the issues in context, so we can truly appreciate the unprecedented power grab that is taking place.

If you really want to roll back the Obama agenda, you must understand who Obama truly is and the motives behind his ruinous policies. Oh, and by all means, feel free to have a laugh at his expense. After all, you've paid for it.

DRAMATIS PERSONAE

BARACK HUSSEIN OBAMA   President of the United States, Community-Organizer-in-Chief, aka "Smokey," Ego Maximus

MICHELLE ROBINSON OBAMA   First Lady of the United States, Fashion Plate, Gardener-in-Chief, Food Czarina, aka "Miche," Ego Magnus

MARIAN ROBINSON   First Grandmother of the United States, mother of Michelle Obama, aka "Mother Robinson," Chief White House babysitter

JOE BIDEN   Vice President of the United States, Master of the Malaprop, Amtrak Guest Rewards Select Plus Member

DESIREE GLAPION ROGERS   White House Social Secretary (February 2009–March 2010), Razzle-Dazzler-in-Chief, Fashionista Extraordinaire, Professional White House dinner guest, former Obama pal

VALERIE JARRETT

Senior Advisor and Assistant to the President, arguably the most influential person in the White House, current Obama pal

REGGIE LOVE

Special Assistant and Personal Aide to the President, Obama's "Body Man," sports and traveling companion

DAVID AXELROD

Senior Advisor to the President, Obama's in-house political strategist, honorary member of D.C.-area Weight Watchers, aka "Axe"

RAHM EMANUEL

White House Chief of Staff, former ballet dancer, Master of the Expletive, House Gym shower habitué

HILLARY RODHAM CLINTON

United States Secretary of State, former First Lady, former Senator, Would-Be President

NANCY PELOSI

Speaker of the United States House of Representatives, California Democratic Congresswoman, self-described "ardent practicing Catholic," Botox cover girl

HARRY REID

Senate Majority Leader, Nevada Democratic Senator, racial healer, often mistaken for elderly mountain woman

TIMOTHY GEITHNER

United States Secretary of the Treasury, TurboTaxEvader

LARRY SUMMERS   Director of the White House National Economic Council, former Secretary of Treasury and Chief Economist of the World Bank

PETER ORSZAG   Director of Office of Management and Budget, aka "Nerdy-Sexy," part-time spokesman for Hair Club for Men, full-time Munchkin voice double

JON FAVREAU   Director of Speechwriting for the White House, former speechwriter for John Kerry, dating Quincy Jones' daughter

ROBERT GIBBS   White House Press Secretary, inveterate babbler, aka "Giblet," "Gibbopotamus," "Gibbotron"

DAVID PLOUFFE   Political consultant and presidential strategist on House and Senate Races, former campaign manager for Obama's 2008 presidential run

THE
OBAMA
DIARIES

THE DIARY OF PRESIDENT BARACK HUSSEIN OBAMA

CHAPTER 1

WHAT IS AMERICA TO ME?

There is an inspiring World War II song, "The House I Live In," that asks:

> *What is America to me?*
> *A name, a map, or a flag I see;*
> *A certain word, democracy.*
> *What is America to me?*

It's a question we don't consider often enough, if at all. But today, a kind of soul searching is needed. Our understanding of America will profoundly shape our actions—and those actions will leave their mark on America and the rest of the world. How we see our country and our role as citizens will either lead us to protect, defend, and nurture her—or sit idly by as our precious heritage slips away.

At this moment in our history, when we face so many challenges at home and abroad, we need to consider anew this crucial question.

What is America to me?

Who are we as Americans? Who do we want to be? What traditions and principles do we need to preserve as we move forward? What of our

American experience is worth fighting for? (And just because you might not wear a military uniform, don't think you are exempt from answering that last question.) These are queries that should be pondered by all Americans and all those who wish to be.

To me, America will always be a land of unbridled opportunity, unrivaled beauty, and unlimited possibility. It is a place where each of us has a shot to reach our potential. Rooted in truth, decency, and timeless values, America is ever forward looking; constantly innovating while inspiring the rest of the world. Echoing John Winthrop (and the Bible), Ronald Reagan captured it best when he described America as "the shining city on a hill." In his farewell address, he unpacked this vision and explained what we are, and must be, in this new millennium:

> In my mind, it was a tall, proud city built on rocks stronger than oceans, wind-swept, God-blessed, and teeming with people of all kinds living in harmony and peace; a city with free ports that hummed with commerce and creativity, and if there had to be city walls, the walls had doors and the doors were open to anyone with the will and the heart to get here. That's how I saw it, and see it still . . . after two hundred years, two centuries, she still stands strong and true on the granite ridge, and her glow has held steady no matter what storm. And she's still a beacon, still a magnet for all who must have freedom, for all the pilgrims from all the lost places who are hurtling through the darkness, toward home.

Just reading the words puts a lump in my throat. Which isn't an isolated occurrence. I also happen to get choked up at ball games. Not by the game itself, but by the National Anthem. Every time I hear it sung or see a stadium full of people with their hands over their hearts, I feel a little tingle. Whenever I spot a veteran standing at attention before a passing flag in a Memorial Day parade, tears inevitably well up in my eyes. It's not sentimentality, but an emotional reaction to this truth: many have sacrificed for what those stars and stripes represent, and the sacrifice continues. How can one help but be moved and humbled by the long trail of blood and sweat that established our "city on a hill" and defended her promise around the world?

Our challenge now, as engaged citizens, is to translate our emotions into clear principles, practices, and habits that rise above the political or cultural winds of the moment. What can we do, personally, to expand the greatness of our country? What steps can we take to extend the sacrifice of those who paid the ultimate price for our freedom to make choices?

I believe that our work needs to begin deep within ourselves. We the people must refine ourselves, as individuals, before we can refine our community and our nation. No one else will do it for us. Not the government, not the media, and certainly not the "international community." We are the ones who will either stand up and defend what we know to be true, or permit others to twist and destroy the last, best hope of mankind. What is at stake is our way of life, our ideals, and our very future.

> *The house I live in,*
> *A plot of earth, a street,*
> *The grocer and the butcher,*
> *Or the people that I meet;*
> *The children in the playground,*
> *The faces that I see,*
> *All races and religions,*
> *That's America to me.*

Like the first settlers in this land, people continue to come to our shores seeking freedom. They embrace and celebrate our ideals in ways that shame native-born Americans. The English writer G. K. Chesterton, in his work *What I Saw in America,* put in this way: "[T]he great American experiment . . . a democracy of diverse races . . . has been compared to a melting-pot. But even that metaphor implies that the pot itself is of a certain shape and a certain substance; a pretty solid substance. The melting-pot must not melt. The original shape was traced on the lines of Jeffersonian democracy; and it will remain in that shape until it becomes shapeless. America invites all men to become citizens; but it implies the dogma that there is such a thing as citizenship."

What gives our country her "shape" is our shared, common belief in what America is. Chesterton observed that we are the only nation founded on a creed. That creed is found in the Declaration of Independence, where Jefferson wrote: "We hold these truths to be self-evident, that all men are created equal" and "that they are endowed by their Creator with certain unalienable Rights, that among these are Life, Liberty and the pursuit of Happiness." Embracing and advancing this vision is at the heart of what it means to be an American. We are not observers in this country, but participants. Citizenship requires that we struggle to protect these ideals of Life, Liberty, and the Pursuit of Happiness. We must all do our part. But the troubling question we face is: Do we all really believe in the American creed?

The Diary of President Barack Obama

Inauguration Night

January 20, 2009

. . . Hell, yes, it's the first time we're proud to be Americans! I can't believe these people actually voted for me! What a place this country is! A measly stint in the Illinois legislature and a breath or two in the Senate, add a few groovy iconic posters and some "Hope & Change" and . . . bingo! I am the f---ing president! They actually bought it when I said I wanted to "form a more perfect union." I think Aretha was crying beneath that Easter basket hat of hers when I said that line . . . hey, I _am_ the perfect union! Good looks, big brains, and a damn fine jump shot at my age.

You should have seen the way Beyoncé looked at me at that ball tonight. Damn! I played it cool though. I didn't even look back at her. I grabbed Michelle's hand, did a few twirls with her in that toilet paper dress, and made my way offstage like a cool cat. They were yelling for me to come back, but I just gave them a wave over the shoulder. I like to leave 'em fired up and ready to go.

Pastor Jeremiah was right; to hell with "America the Beautiful." It's the era of Barack the Beautiful. Long may I reign.

Unfortunately for Americans, the leader of the United States and his intimates have a deeply distorted view of America. Throw in unhealthy doses of class warfare, envy, and narcissism, and the long-cherished vision of America becomes almost unrecognizable—like Nancy Pelosi after a long Botox session.

Leaders from George Washington to Teddy Roosevelt to Ronald Reagan celebrated this country apart from themselves; praising her virtues, her ideals. President Obama takes a different tack. To understand where he is coming from and where he means to take us, it helps to look back.

In March 2008, while on the campaign trail, then-senator Obama offered this touching salute to America: ". . . for as long as I live, I will never forget that in no other country on earth is *my story* even possible."

No matter the topic, no matter the occasion, whenever Barack Obama is talking, rest assured that the oration will somehow relate back to *him*! His personal narrative is always in evidence. Like Rome, all roads lead to Barry. Even America and her long, noble history must bend to accommodate the "story" of Barack Obama. But at least he is consistent. He always sings in the same key: Me, Me, Me, Me, Me . . .

Michelle and Barack Obama have a truly lamentable track record when it comes to celebrating America as the greatest country on the face of the earth. Probably because they don't believe it's true. Now, for those who think I am being petty—with apologies to the president—let me be clear: I've been around politics long enough to know, if you want to understand what a person really thinks and feels, don't listen to the scripted speech. Listen when they speak off the cuff. Listen for what they don't say. The truth is far more likely to come tumbling out when the teleprompter is off. And it has tumbled out.

On February 18, 2008, at a campaign rally in Madison, Wisconsin, Michelle Obama uttered the now-infamous proclamation about America: "For the first time in my adult lifetime, I am really proud of my country—and not just because Barack has done well, but because I think people are hungry for change. And I have been desperate to see our country moving in that direction and not just feeling so alone in my frustration and disappointment."

"For the first time in my adult lifetime, I am really proud of my country . . ."

Can you imagine reaching the age of forty-four and never having been proud of your country? Michelle Obama couldn't find one American virtue or laudable quality that stirred pride in her heart in all those years? Worse, she added that she was frustrated and disappointed in the country. Like her husband, the First Lady saw no objective goodness in America until they arrived on the scene.

During the 2008 campaign, Lauren Collins profiled Michelle Obama for the *New Yorker*. She wrote: "[Michelle] Obama begins with a broad assessment of life in America in 2008, and life is not good: we're a divided country, we're a country that is 'just downright mean,' we are 'guided by fear,' we're a nation of cynics, sloths, and complacents."

I have often tried to figure out why it is that liberals—especially Ivy League–educated liberals—have such a hard time loving America unconditionally. Whether it is a multimillionaire actor like Sean Penn or a business tycoon émigré like George Soros, our country's most privileged liberal elites seem genetically predisposed to think the worst about the country that helped them achieve their wealth and celebrity. Why is this? What other country on the planet is better, freer, more beautiful than ours? (Both would probably scoff at the previous sentence for its "mindless flag-waving sentimentality.")

Surely, as individuals, we can be critical of our political leadership—Lord knows I am—yet at the same time love our country and be grateful for the sacrifices of our forefathers. While I can certainly understand one having a dim view of certain political figures or events, I cannot understand the overall negative, cynical view shared by so many Obama boosters. You know the mind-set—the type who reflexively feel the need to remind the world that America has screwed up royally.

For them, America is better now only because it has embraced the Obamas. But by any measure, America is a great country. She was magnificent and set apart before the Obamas came along and will continue to be "the shining city on the hill" long after they are gone.

THE DIARY OF FIRST LADY MICHELLE OBAMA

THE WHITE HOUSE

January 21, 2009

I've got to tell you, making history is exhausting. After the parade and the balls and the Jonas Brothers' drop-by, I am now stuck in this drafty, <u>white</u> mausoleum of a house, arranging bedrooms! I'd like to see Barack get five people situated in a new house overnight.

This morning, I'm sitting with Mama at the breakfast table in my robe, just worn out, and Barack walks in all spiffed up, giving me that "The First Lady have big plans today?" jazz. I threw my newspaper down, looked him straight in the eye, and said, "Listen, buddy, you go arrange the girls' bedrooms and I'll go meet with the national security team, okay? Believe me, that's easier. And I probably know more about national security than you!"

He didn't say a word. When he tried to quietly slink away, Mama gave him the evil eye and said, real loud, "This First Lady's got bigger plans than you'll _ever_ have, string bean!" Even the servants were laughing.

I begged those Bushes to let us stay at Blair House, the White House guest residence, after the election and bring our things in slowly. But noooo! They had "dignitaries to accommodate." So we were cooped up like refugees over at the Hay-Adams. (Do you know they didn't even have conditioner in the bathroom?) The Bushes should have gotten the hell out of this house in November after the election and let us move in. We're historic! Mrs. Literacy and Mr. Illiterate should have gone to a hotel. Didn't they already have their eight years?

After I unpack Sasha's room, I've got to get dressed and go to some damn military thing. Just what I need today. All that flag-waving, hillbilly music, hand-on-the-heart crap. To think that for the next four years I have to ooh and aah over the "sacrifice" of people who never graduated college . . . You want to know what sacrifice is? Giving up a cushy, six-figure, hospital board salary to play second fiddle to a man who still leaves his dirty socks in the middle of the bedroom floor.

But Desiree says, as First Lady, I've got to distance myself from the "first time I'm proud of my country" comments. So here I go: hugging and saluting and singing "Yankee Doodle Dandy"—again! Desiree picked out a blue sheath dress with a stars-and-stripes bow on the front. And I've got to say, my arms look fine in it. If I play my cards right, I might get an <u>American Legion</u> magazine cover out of this thing.

> The place I work in,
> The worker by my side,
> The little town or city
> Where my people lived and died.
> The howdy and the handshake,
> The air and feeling free,
> And the right to speak my mind out,
> That's America to me.

How we speak of our country, how we treat the symbols of our freedom, the gratitude we show to our military and veterans—all of this defines who we are as Americans. Words and gestures, even the things we wear, express in a concrete way what's in our hearts. A big part of patriotism is showing everyone we meet that we believe in the American creed—that we are proud of this country and her history, regardless of her shortcomings. President Obama has disparaged such displays. As a senator and presidential candidate, he made a point of removing his flag lapel pin in 2007.

"The truth is that right after 9/11, I had a pin. Shortly after 9/11, particularly because as we're talking about the Iraq War, that became a substitute for, I think, true patriotism, which is speaking out on issues that are of importance to our national security," Obama said in Cedar Rapids, Iowa, that year. "I decided I won't wear that pin on my chest. Instead I'm going to try to tell the American people what I believe, what will make this country great, and hopefully, that will be a testimony to my patriotism."

So Obama is going to tell the American people "what will make this country great." You'd swear he was a coach positioning himself to save a losing team—as if the country isn't great now, but after it adopts *his* agenda, it will be spectacular. No wonder he would later attempt to, in his words, "fundamentally transform the United States of America."

Obama is simply wrong. Our patriotism, our devotion to country, should never be swayed by the passing policies of the government. I agree with Mark Twain, who wrote, "Patriotism is supporting your country all the time, and your government when it deserves it." I would argue that the lapel pin and displays like it are an outgrowth of our patriotism, tangible signs of faith in America.

Obama's lapel-pin comments drew a firestorm of criticism, prompting him to further dismiss the importance of such displays in (ironically) Independence, Iowa: "After a while, you start noticing people wearing a lapel pin, but not acting very patriotic. Not voting to provide veterans with resources that they need. Not voting to make sure that disability payments are coming out on time. My attitude is that I'm less concerned about what you're wearing on your lapel than what's in your heart."

Who knew that among Obama's many gifts was the reading of hearts? To defuse the controversy, Obama began wearing the flag pin throughout the campaign and continues wearing it today. What, then, does the pin on his lapel actually mean, given his admitted feelings?

Barack Obama's flawed thinking about America and how to present her to the world has now bled into his presidency, with disastrous results.

WHY WE'RE GREAT

Born of our revolutionary spirit and belief in the Almighty, America has long seen itself as exceptional—a people and a land set apart. Alexis de Tocqueville was the first to call America "exceptional." But the principle has been enlarged and confirmed by our astounding growth and leadership in the world for more than two centuries.

The *Encyclopedia of American Foreign Policy* describes American exceptionalism as "a term used to describe the belief that the United States is an extraordinary nation with a special role to play in human history; a nation that is not only unique but also superior." Our national pride and confidence come from this notion of American exceptionalism. It gives America the strength to seek out those things that are in her best interests and in the best interests of those in other lands.

If you have traveled outside the country for any length of time, you know there is nothing like coming home to the United States. That doesn't mean there aren't problems (like going through customs), but when one returns from a trip abroad, the marks of our exceptionalism are more apparent than ever by contrast. In the power of our industry. In the self-reliant, independent spirit of our people. The generosity of Americans. Their concern for their fellow man and the common good. These are the qualities that define us. (Just look at the outpouring of support for the people of Haiti during their recent tragedies—in the midst of a recession, I might add.) The proof of America's exceptionalism is in evidence for anyone with eyes to see it.

> *The things I see about me,*
> *The big things and the small,*
> *The little corner newsstand,*
> *And the house a mile tall;*
> *The wedding and the churchyard,*
> *The laughter and the tears,*
> *And the dream that's been a growing*
> *For more than two hundred years.*

It is obvious from our founding documents that the Framers considered America exceptional as well. They saw us as a people led by Providence, rooted in the ideals of equality under the law and freedom for all. Somewhere along the way, President Obama must have missed that lesson in history class. When asked about American exceptionalism at the NATO conference in April 2009, the leader of the free world said:

> I believe in American exceptionalism, just as I suspect that the Brits believe in British exceptionalism and the Greeks believe in Greek exceptionalism. . . . Now, the fact that I am very proud of my country and I think that we've got a whole lot to offer the world does not lessen my interest in recognizing the value and wonderful qualities of other countries, or recognizing that we're not always going to be right, or that other people may have good ideas, or that in order for us to work collectively, all parties have to compromise and that includes us.

Inspiring, isn't it?

Just one day before, at the G-20 summit on April 2, 2009, in London, the president offered this nugget: "I do not buy into the notion that America can't lead in the world, but it is very important for us to be able to forge partnerships as opposed to dictating solutions."

Notice the language: in Obama's worldview, before he came on the scene America was a dictator, a bully—"downright mean." This perspective serves only to dilute the moral authority and influence of the United States and embolden the world's true dictators. Obama thinks he's being the sophisticated anti-Bush by offering foreign nations greater opportunities for "dialogue and understanding." But, of course, the result is the diminishment of America's leverage and strength in the world. No wonder they all think they can roll us now.

Throughout the NATO and the G-20 summits of 2009, Europe set the ground rules and led the way. Which was hardly a surprise. It was exactly what the president desired. When he first arrived at the G-20, he told British prime minister Gordon Brown that he had come "to listen, not to lecture." At a press conference with German chancellor Angela Merkel at